AMELIA

ALONE ACROSS
the
OCEAN

Published in Australia by Weldon Kids Pty Ltd
Unit 4, 9 Apollo Street, Warriewood, 2102, Australia
A member of the Weldon International Group of Companies

First published 1996

Chief executive: Leonie Weldon
Project manager: Leah Walsh
Designed by Cheryl Orsini
Printed in Australia by McPhersons Print Group

© Weldon Kids Pty Ltd

National Library of Australia Cataloguing-in-publication data

Young, Leonie
Amelia Earhart - alone across the ocean.

ISBN 1 875875 14 X

1. Earhart, Amelia, 1897-1937 - Journeys - Juvenile fiction.
I. Janks, Avril. II. Riddle, Tohby. III. Title.

A823.3

All rights reserved. Subject to the Copyright Act 1968, no part of this publication may be reproduced, stored in a retrieval system, or transmitted in any form, or by any means, electronic, mechanical, photocopying, recording, or otherwise, without prior written permission of the publisher.

AMELIA EARHART

ALONE ACROSS
the
OCEAN

Written by Leonie Young and Avril Janks
Illustrated by Tohby Riddle

WELDON
KiDS

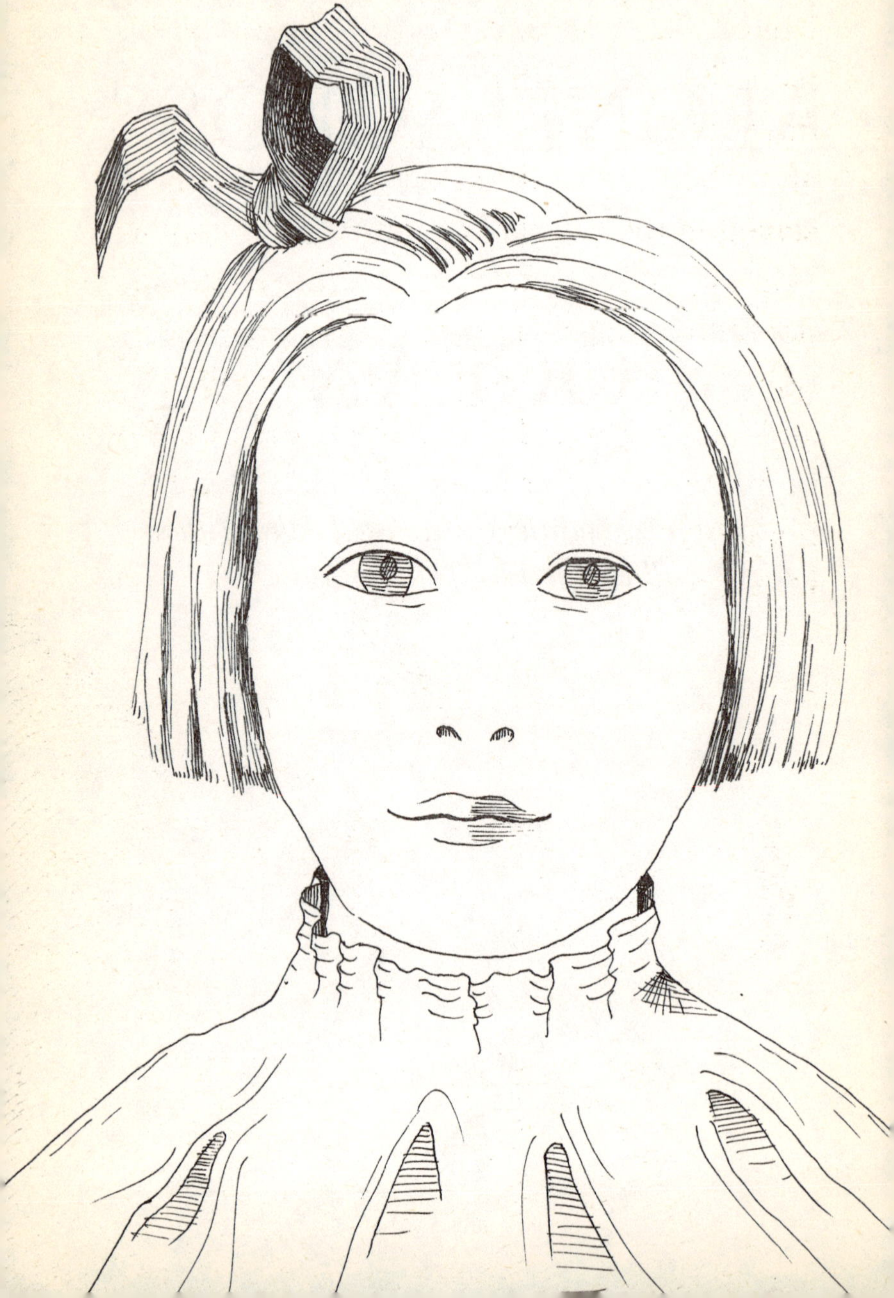

About a hundred years ago in Kansas in the United States of America, there lived a girl named Amelia Earhart. Her parents had to travel often because of her father's work, and when they did Amelia and her sister stayed in the country with their grandmother.

Being in the country meant Amelia could do all the things she loved - climbing trees, riding sleds down steep hills, playing ball and jumping over fences. She was constantly in trouble with her grandmother, who felt her behaviour was far too boisterous for a little girl.

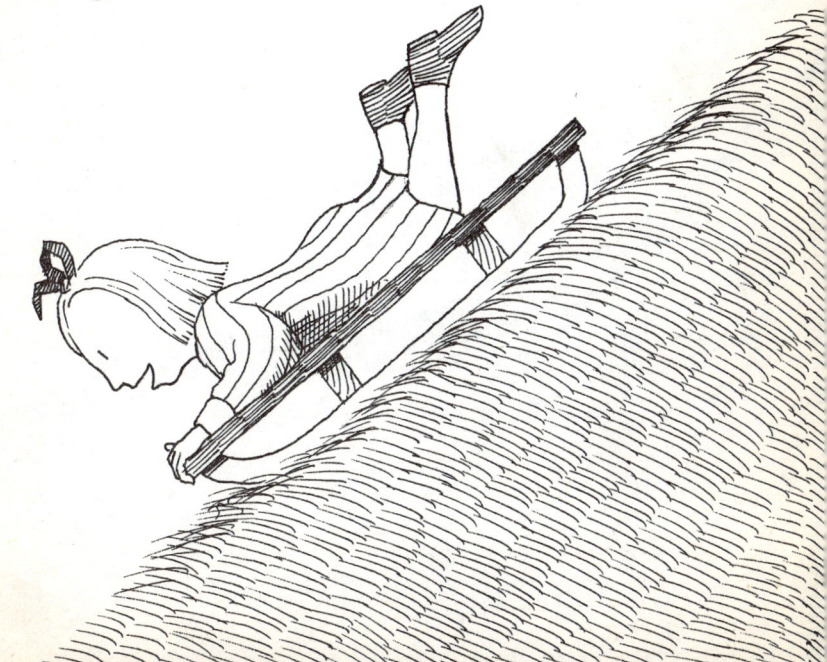

One day, after visiting a fair, Amelia decided to build her own rollercoaster. She carefully planned her design and convinced her uncle to help with its construction. It ran from the roof of the toolshed down to the backyard. Amelia was thrilled. Not only was it complete, it also worked.

Her parents, however, were not so thrilled, and that night as Amelia slept they took the rollercoaster to pieces, feeling it was far too dangerous for a little girl.

All the grown-ups in Amelia's life kept trying to discourage her yearning for speed and danger. But Amelia was Amelia, and she continued to fill her days with dreams of adventure and to read action stories, imagining herself as the hero.

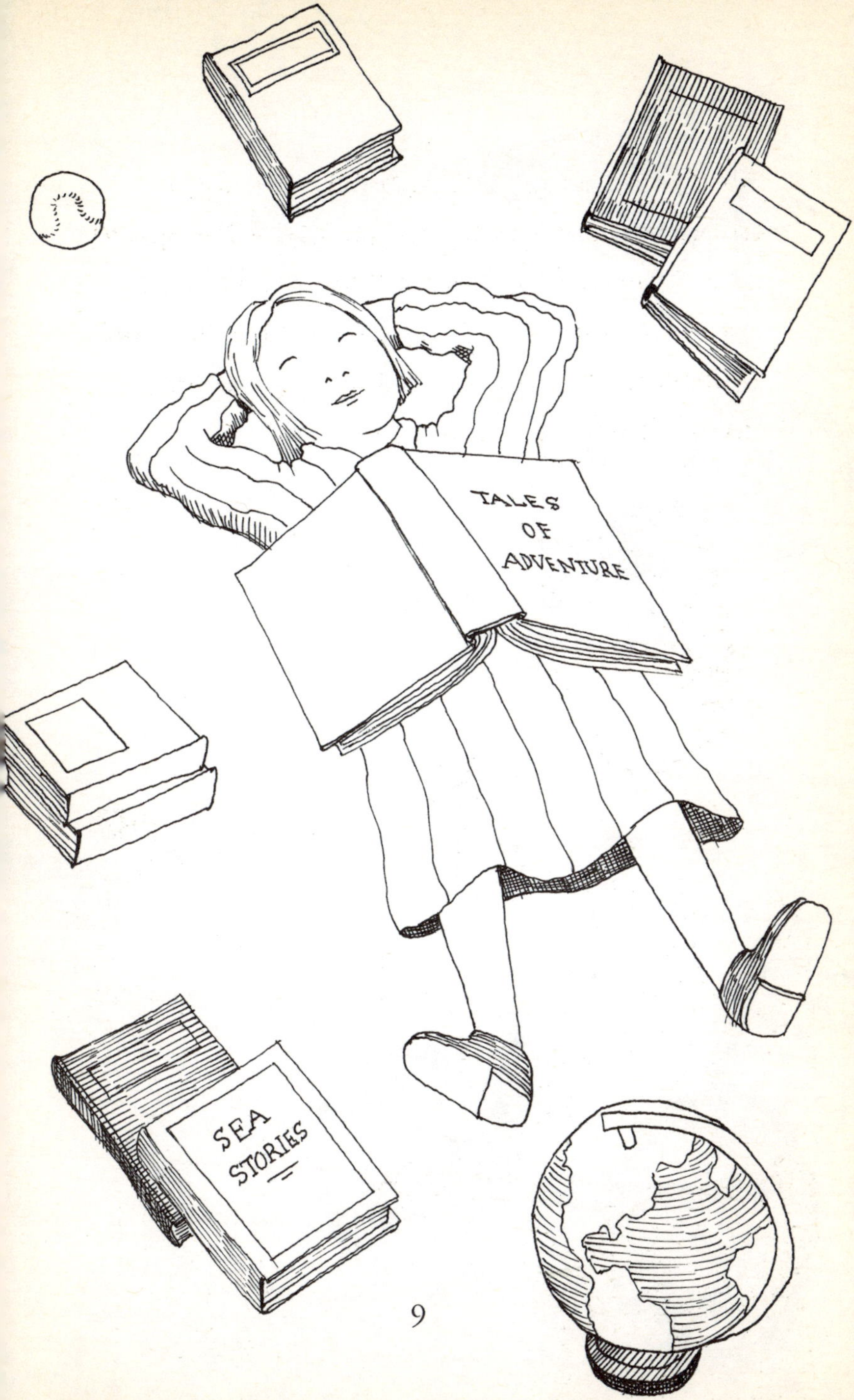
TALES OF ADVENTURE
SEA STORIES

10

When she was ten years old, Amelia saw her first plane - and she was not impressed. It was a rusty, rattly, dilapidated old craft, and hardly looked like a machine she would choose for adventure. 'I'd prefer to ride head-first down a hill on my sled!' she thought.

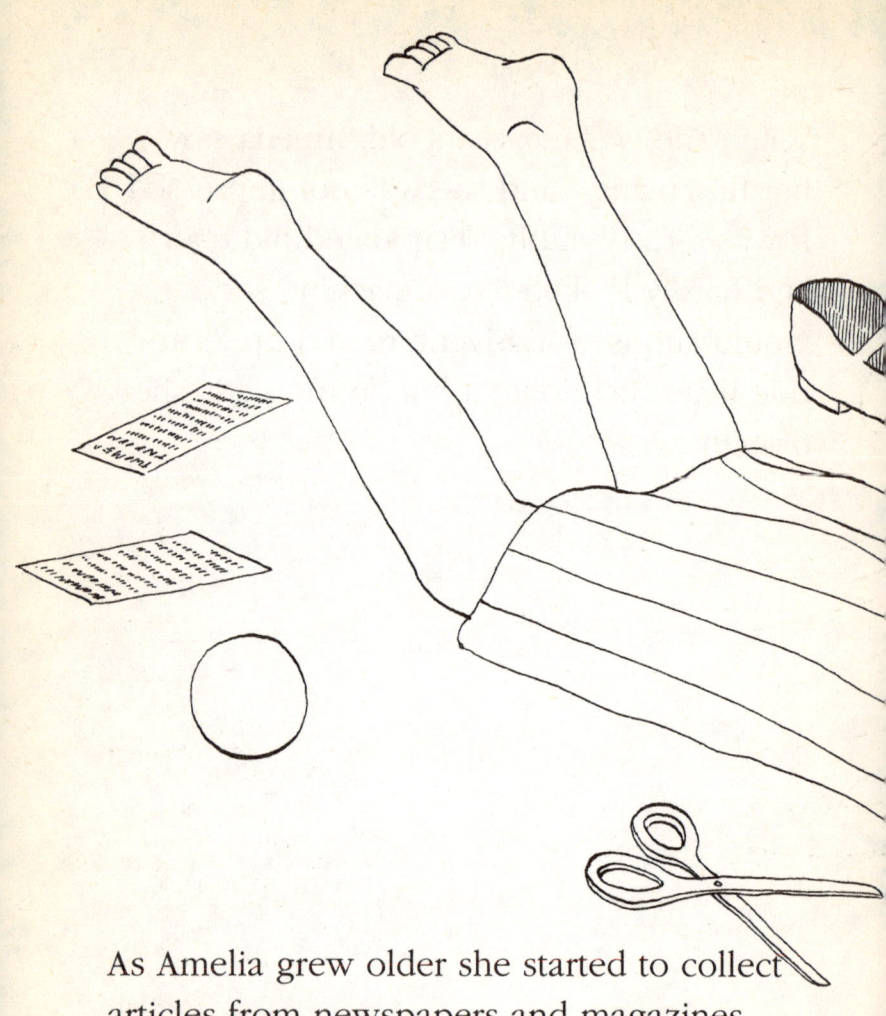

As Amelia grew older she started to collect articles from newspapers and magazines about women who had unusual jobs or lived in interesting places. Flicking through her scrapbook, she often wondered what exciting things she might end up doing some day.

GLU
FOREIGN WOMEN DEVELOPING AS FILM DIRECTORS
WOMAN WANTS TO
CITIES WANT WOMEN POLICE
MODERN WOMAN AGAIN BREAKS TRADITION

14

One day, a few years later, something happened that changed Amelia's life forever. She was at an airfield, where pilots were doing aerobatics, turning upside down and going into loop-the-loops. There was a little red plane that seemed to be special. It flew so low she could feel the power of the engine roar past her.

Amelia couldn't keep her eyes off this plane. It almost seemed to say something to her. She would never forget it. From that moment on, all she wanted to do was fly!

The fact that in those days most people had never set foot in a plane made Amelia even more determined.

Earning money for expensive flying lessons was the first step. She took any work she could find, from nursing and child care to truck driving and selling sausages.

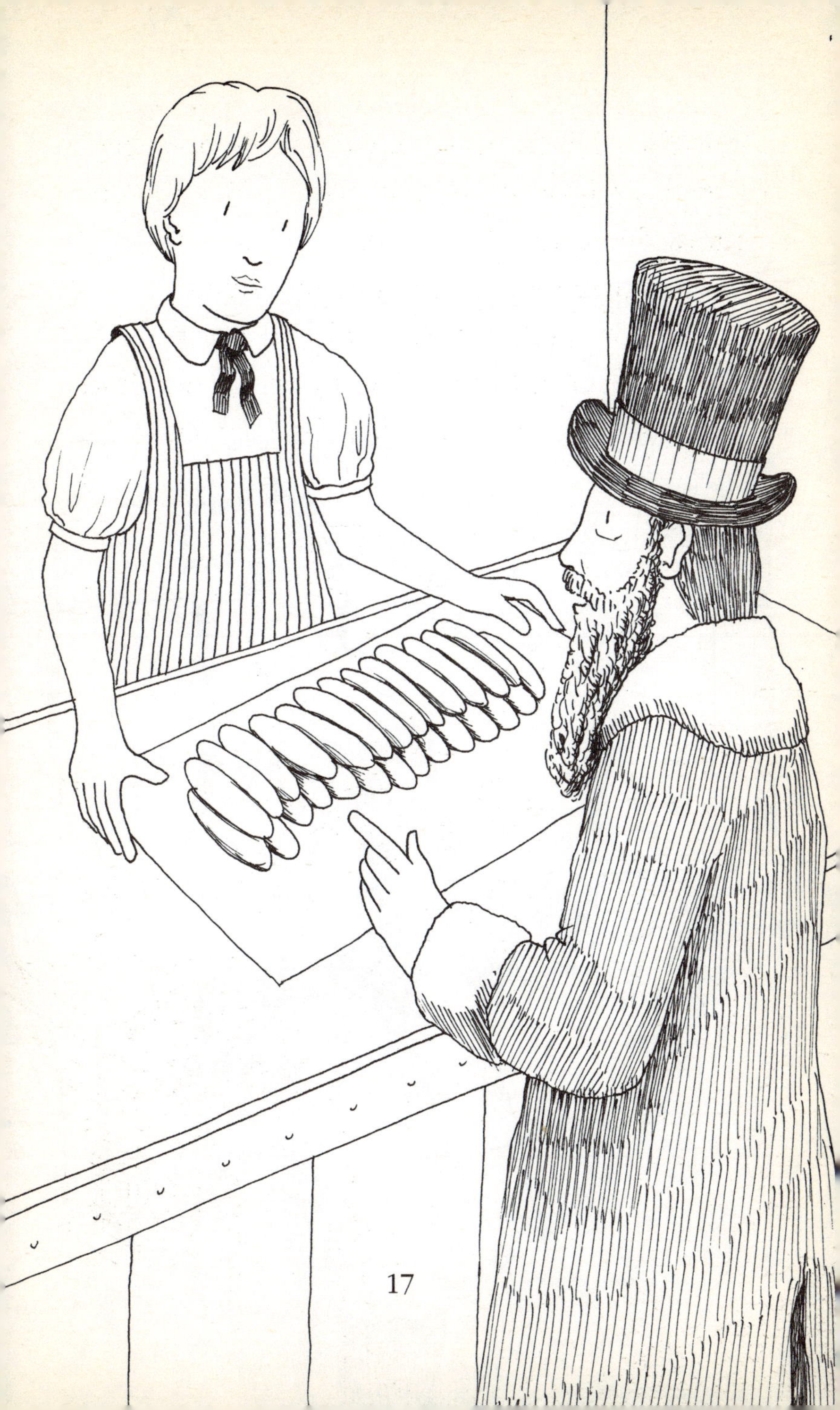

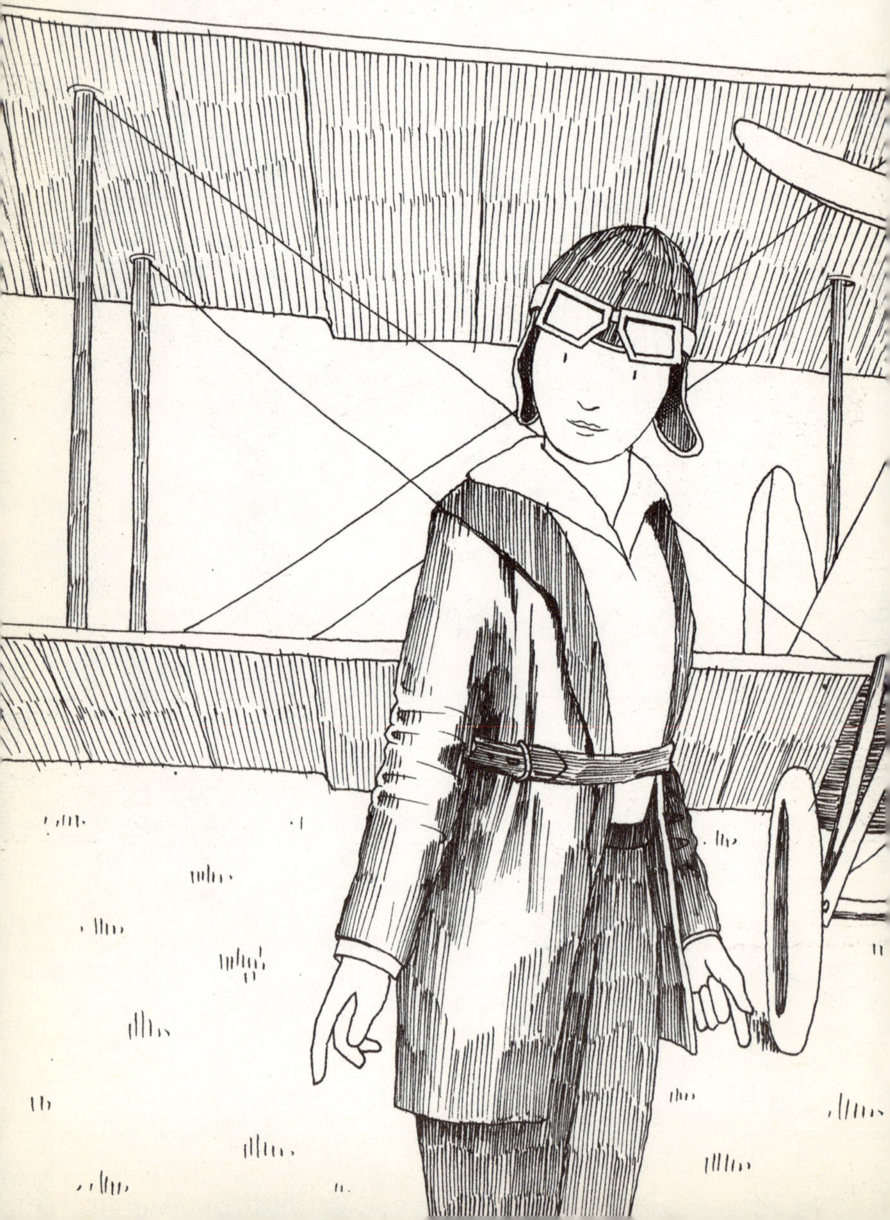

Amelia worked hard. She got her pilot's licence, and even bought her own plane. It was yellow, and she named it 'Canary'.

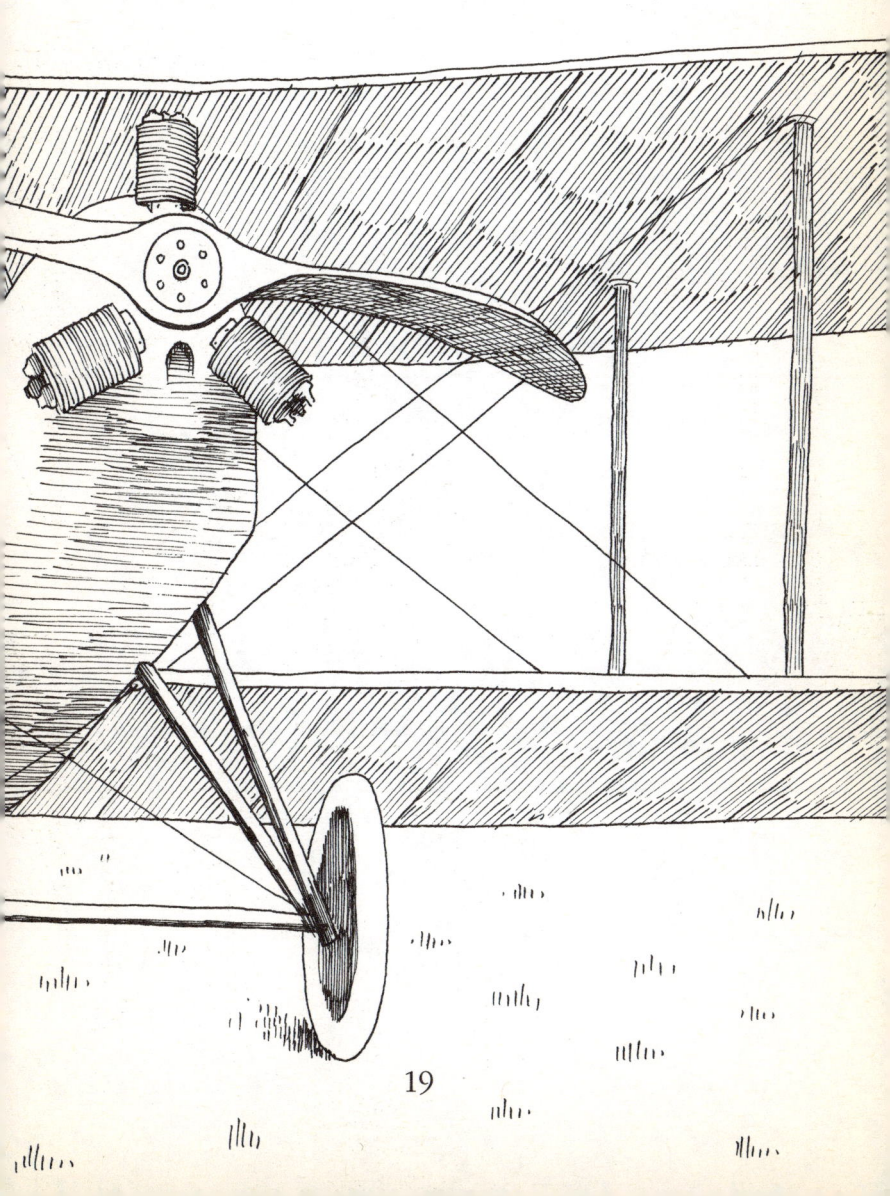

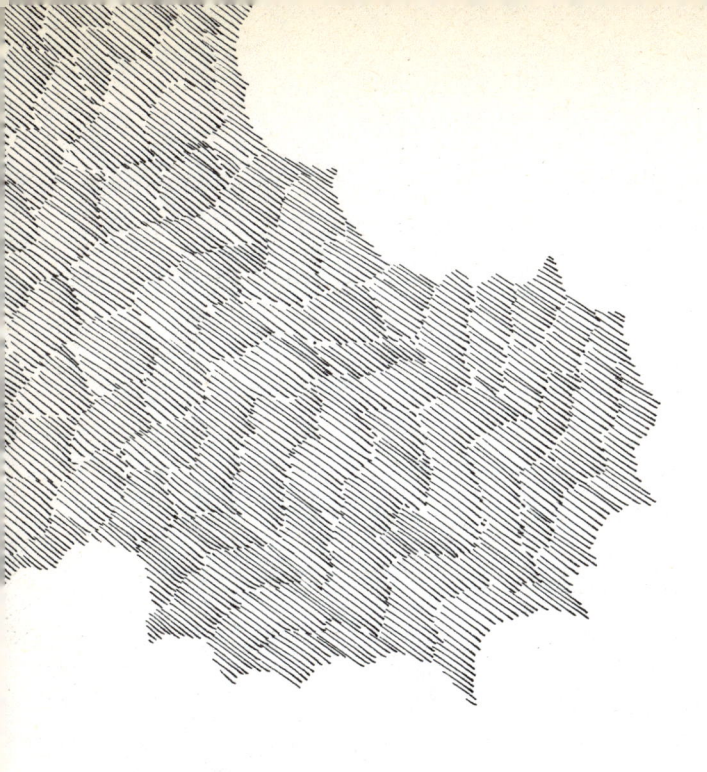

Amelia loved flying more than she had ever dreamed. In no time at all she was up to her old tricks. 'I wonder what Grandma would say now?' she thought as she pushed the plane to its limits, flying as fast and as high as she could. When she took her plane to 14 000 feet, Amelia made the record for flying higher than any other woman.

She continued working in odd jobs to pay for fuel and repairs to her plane. By the age of 29, Amelia had had 28 different jobs.

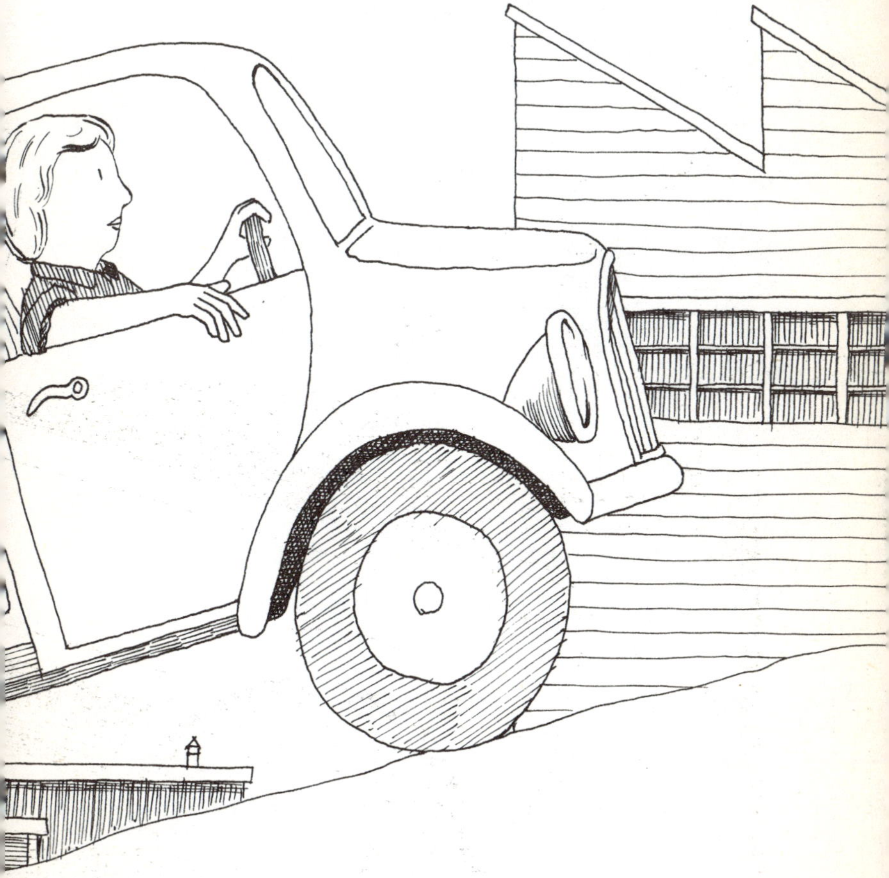

People started to hear more and more about Amelia - one of them was George Palmer Putnam, a successful publisher and promoter, who was organising an historic flight across the Atlantic Ocean. For the first time, a crew would fly from America to England taking a woman passenger with them. Mr Putnam asked Amelia to be the passenger on the plane, which they called the 'Friendship'.

This would make her the first woman ever to fly across this vast, empty ocean. 'Now this sounds like a great adventure,' thought Amelia, and quickly agreed.

Only five planes had ever flown across the Atlantic before. In those days anybody travelling by plane across a vast stretch of water with nowhere to land was considered very brave.

Amelia met the pilot and navigator, and grew more and more excited as the time for their departure grew closer. The 'Friendship' was a deep orange seaplane with gold wings, and was the largest plane Amelia had ever been in.

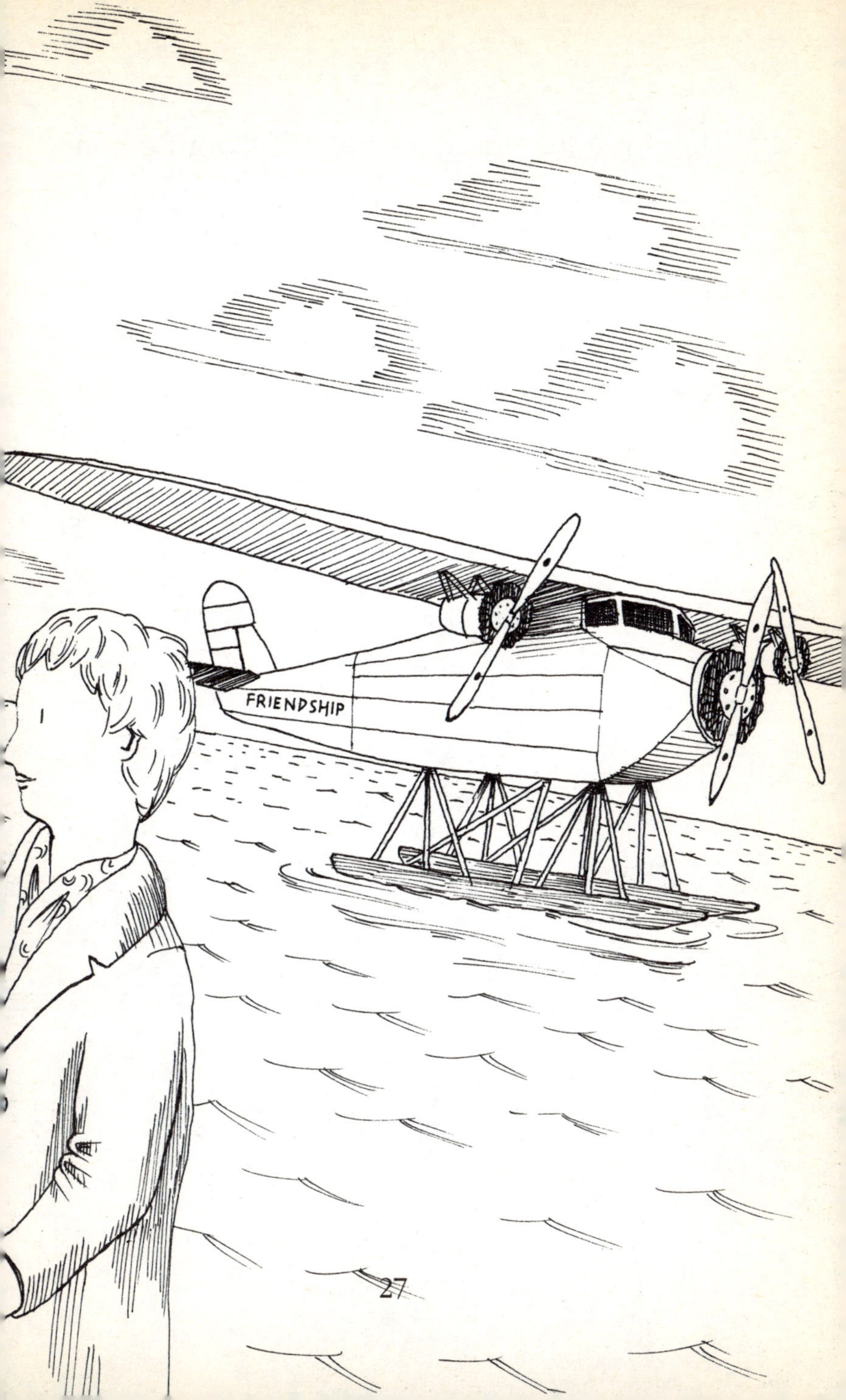
FRIENDSHIP

The three adventurers took off from Boston, but had to stop in Newfoundland on the east coast of Canada because of rain. Finally they left, flying through thick cloud. The fuel ran dangerously low, but Amelia never let either the pilot or the navigator lose hope.

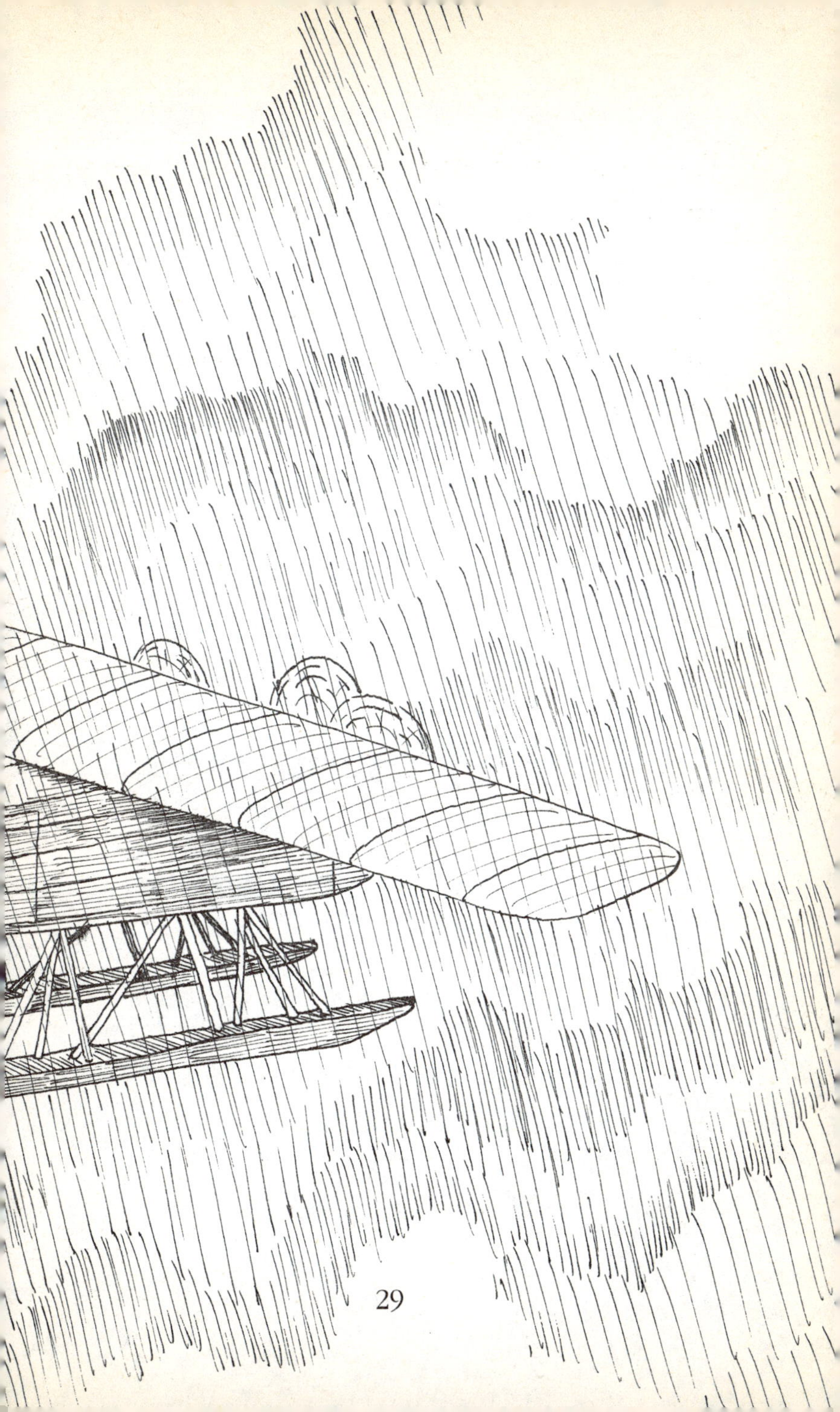

30

When the 'Friendship' finally touched down safely in Wales in the UK, thousands of people surrounded the plane to see the heroes for themselves.

The New York Times
AMELIA EARHART FIRST WOMAN TO CROSS THE ATLANTIC. AMELIA AND 'FRIENDSHIP' CREW PARADE TODAY.

The flight made Amelia world famous.
People found her fascinating, and she soon
became their hero. She appeared in
newspapers and magazines all around the
world, just like the women in her scrapbook.

She wrote a book about the flight and articles on flying in magazines for women.

She travelled across America for weeks at a time, talking to audiences about her adventure. She was also asked to advertise all kinds of products. People got used to seeing her picture everywhere.

But Amelia was restless. She knew that she wanted to do more than just be a famous passenger, and was eager to prove she could be a great pilot too. She flew in air races and broke many speed records.

But she knew there was an adventure that would prove her skills and bravery more than any other. 'I'm going to cross the Atlantic again,' she decided, 'but this time as the pilot, and on my own.'

She worked furiously for two months, planning and checking, preparing for her brave flight. She would leave from Newfoundland, and try to land in either France or Britain on the other side of the huge Atlantic Ocean.

The plane had to be fitted with extra fuel tanks, because there was nowhere for her to land for refuelling along the route. She also had expensive instruments installed, including an altimeter, so she would always know how high she was flying - even if clouds filled the sky and she couldn't see for herself.

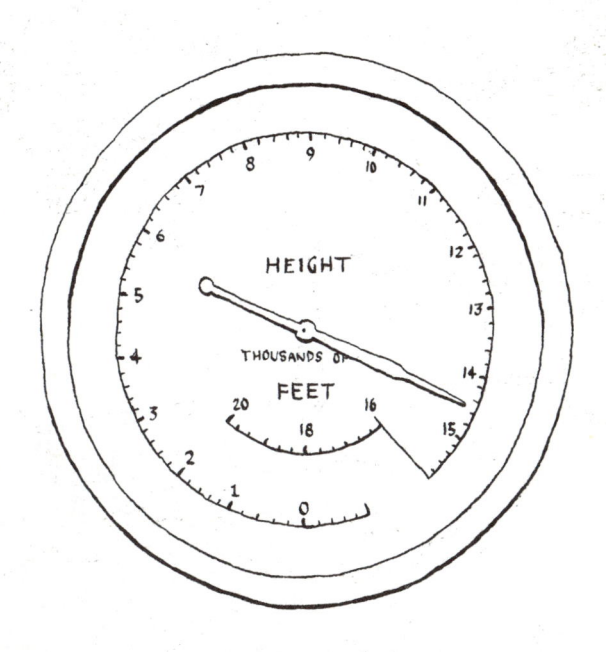

Altimeter.

The day of the flight finally arrived. Amelia took off at sunset on the 20th of May 1932. There was no crowd to wish her good luck. She didn't want people to know about her flight until she was safely on the other side.

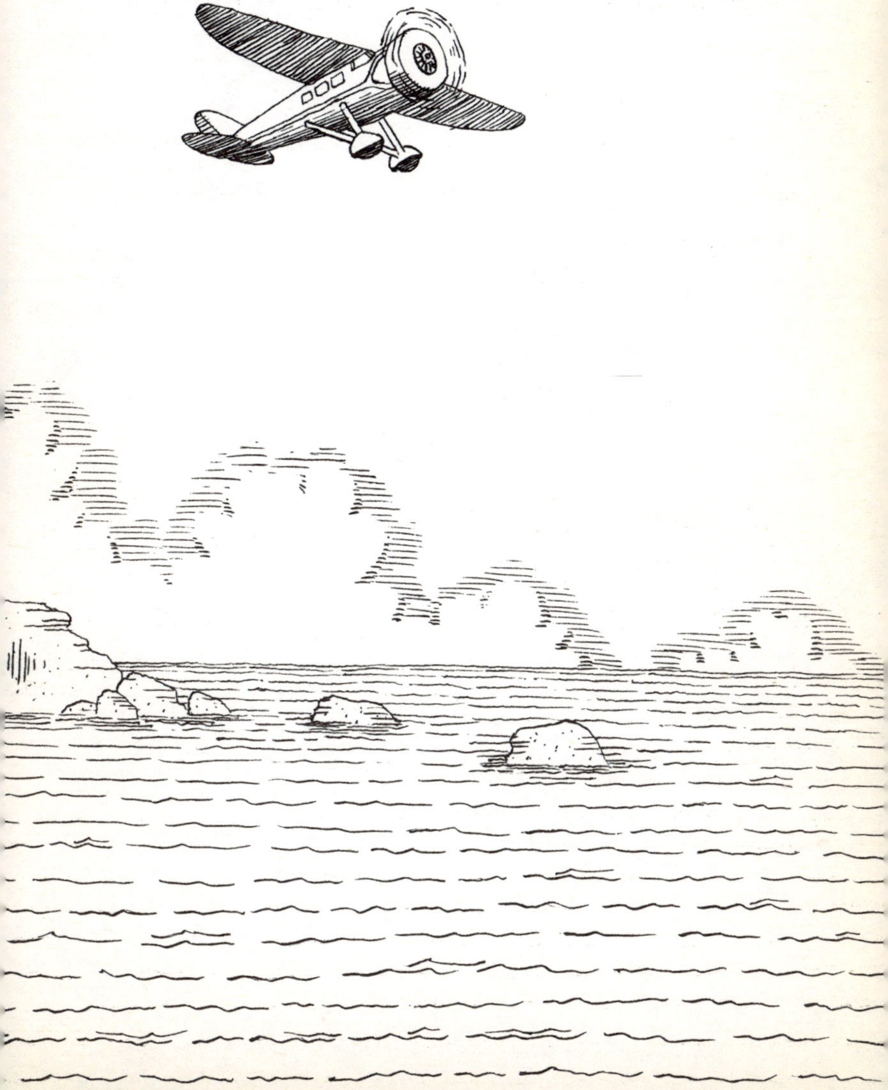

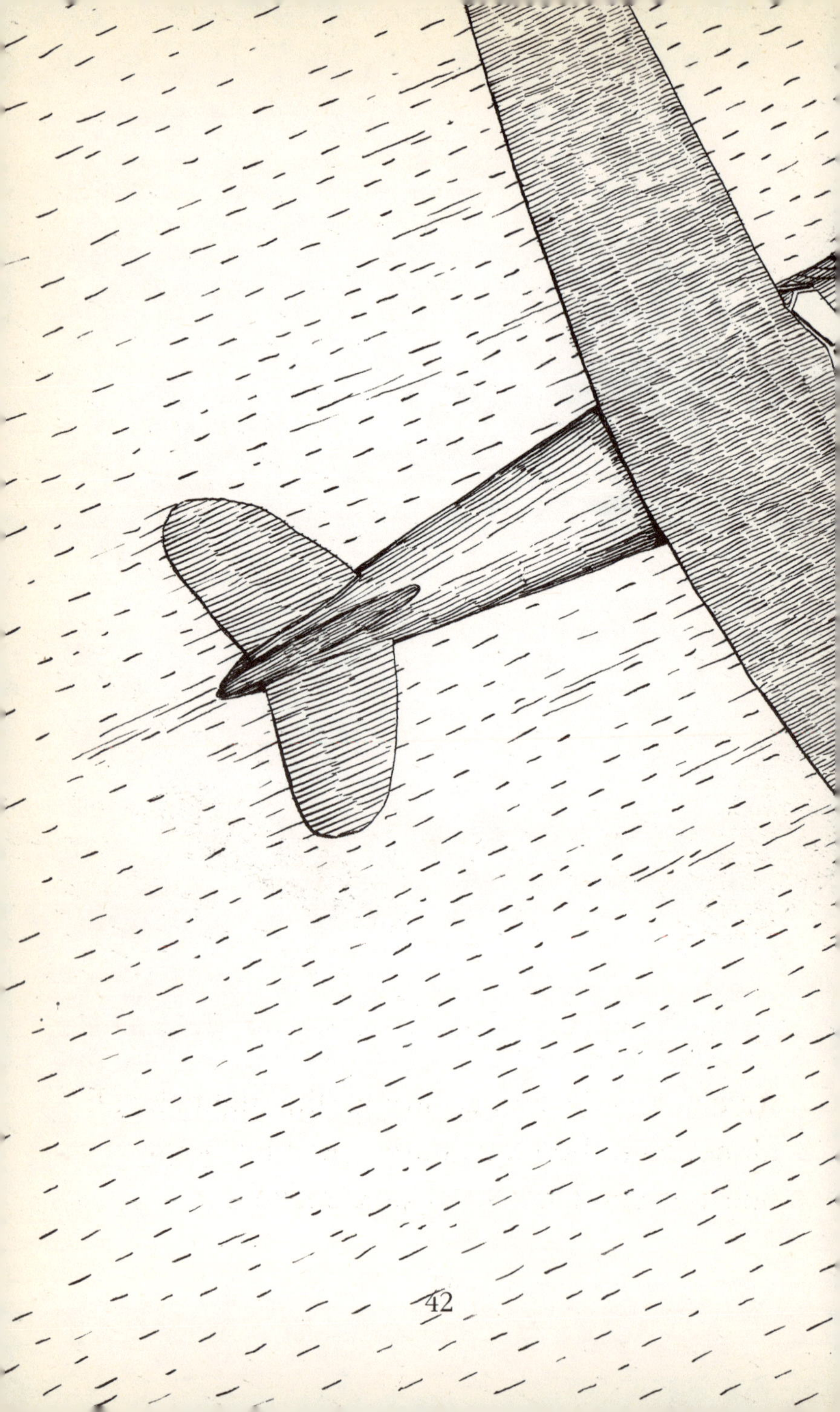

Amelia loved soaring through the night sky all alone, with the huge, dark ocean far below. She was confident she would make it.

But, all too soon, just before midnight, the weather started to change and she was suddenly surrounded by an angry storm.

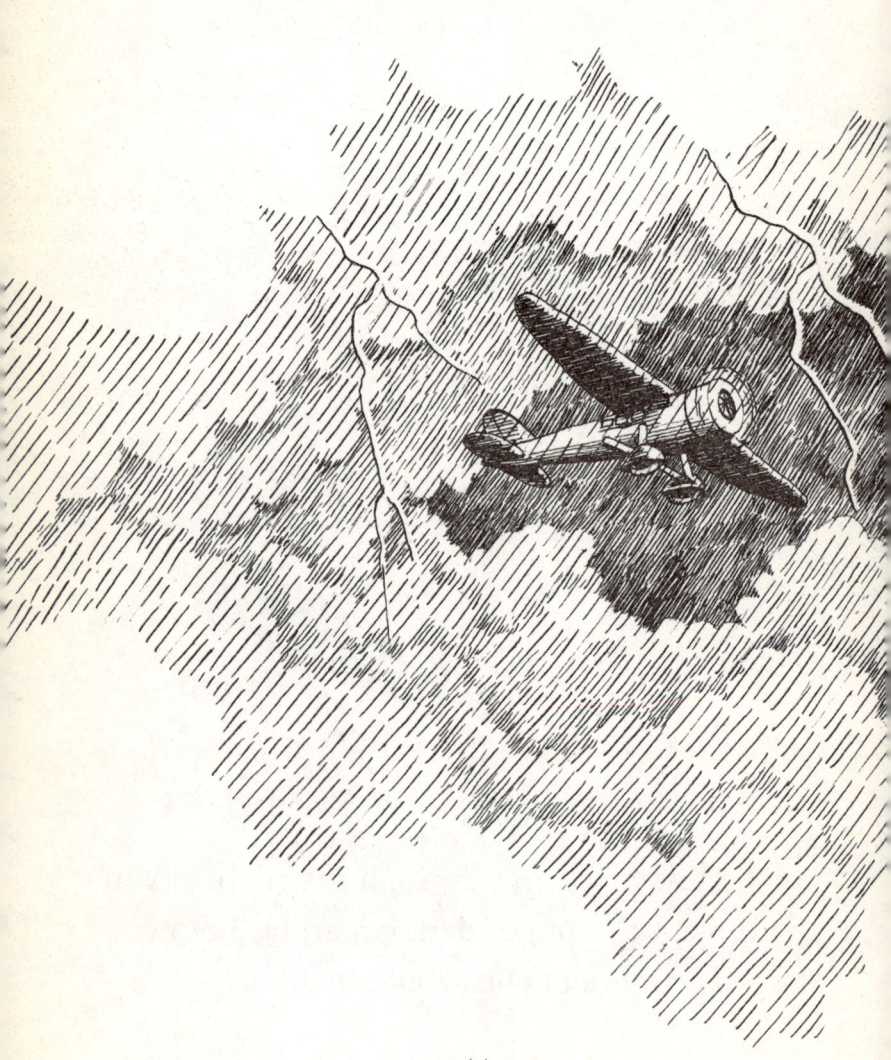

The rain was so fierce she could hardly see, and Amelia felt very fragile as the thunder crashed around her. Lightning lit up the angry sky and the plane was battered back and forth like paper in the strong winds.

The vital altimeter broke, which meant she had no way of telling if she was flying too low. She pulled back hard on the joystick and flew the plane higher to rise above the storm clouds. Flames had started to appear from her engine.

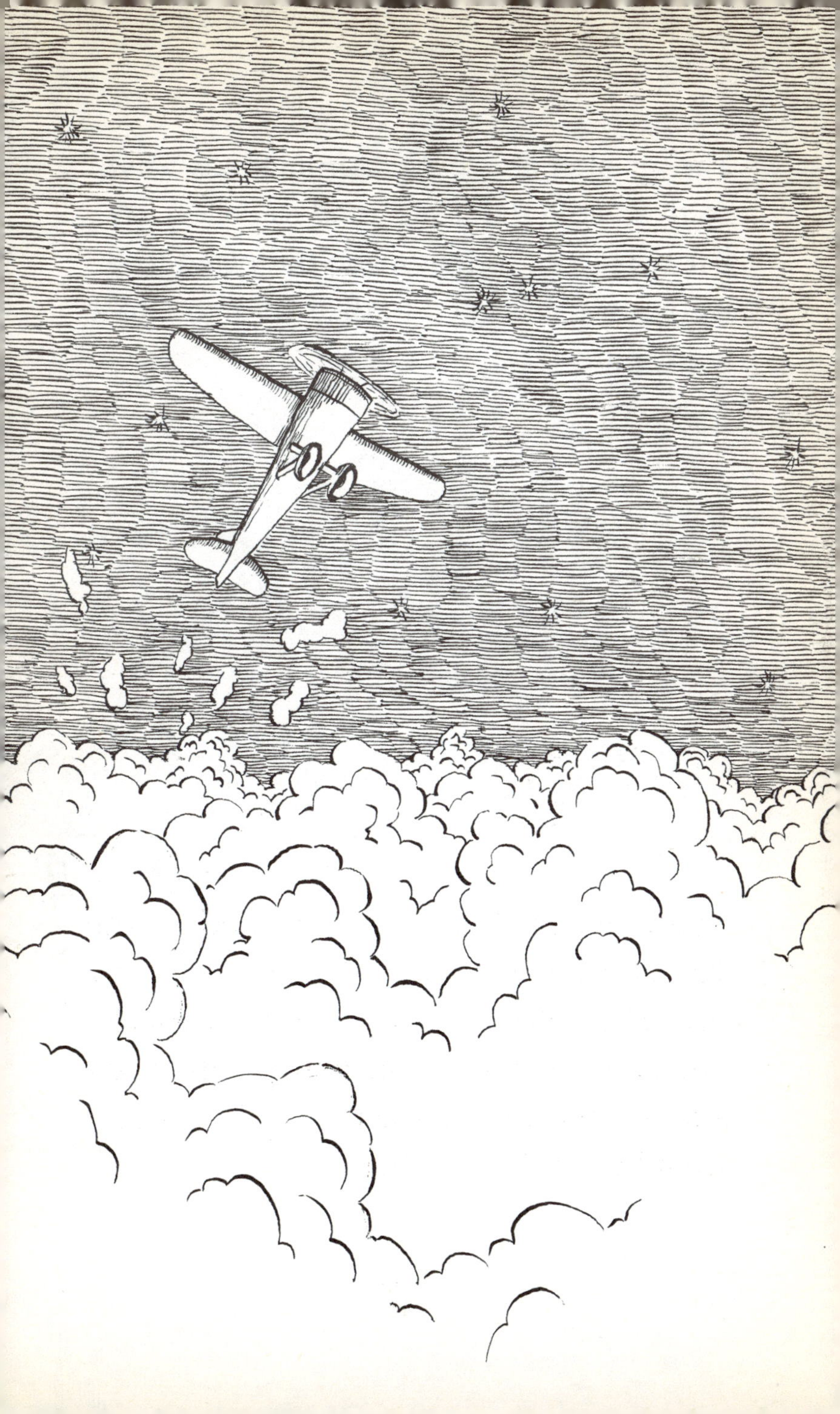

The air high above the storm clouds was cold, so cold that ice started to collect on her wings. Its weight made the plane lose its balance. It started to dive, and go into a mad spin …

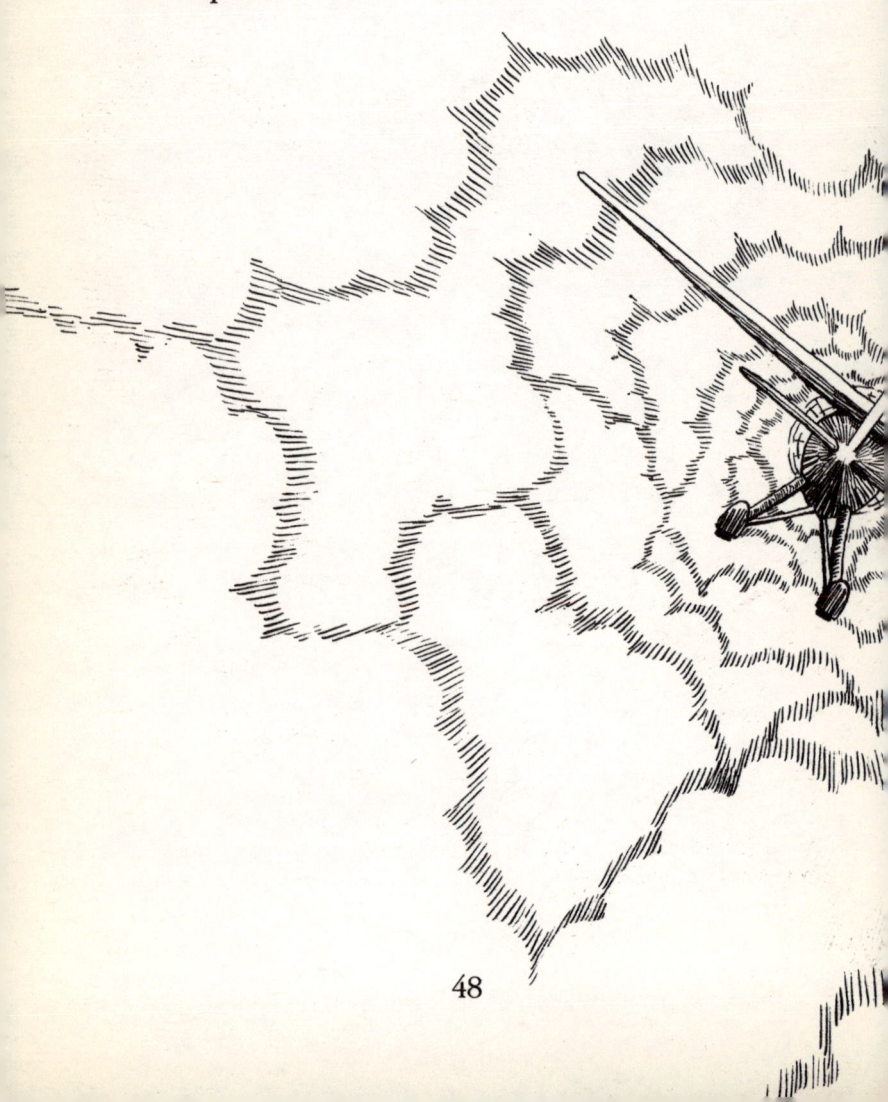

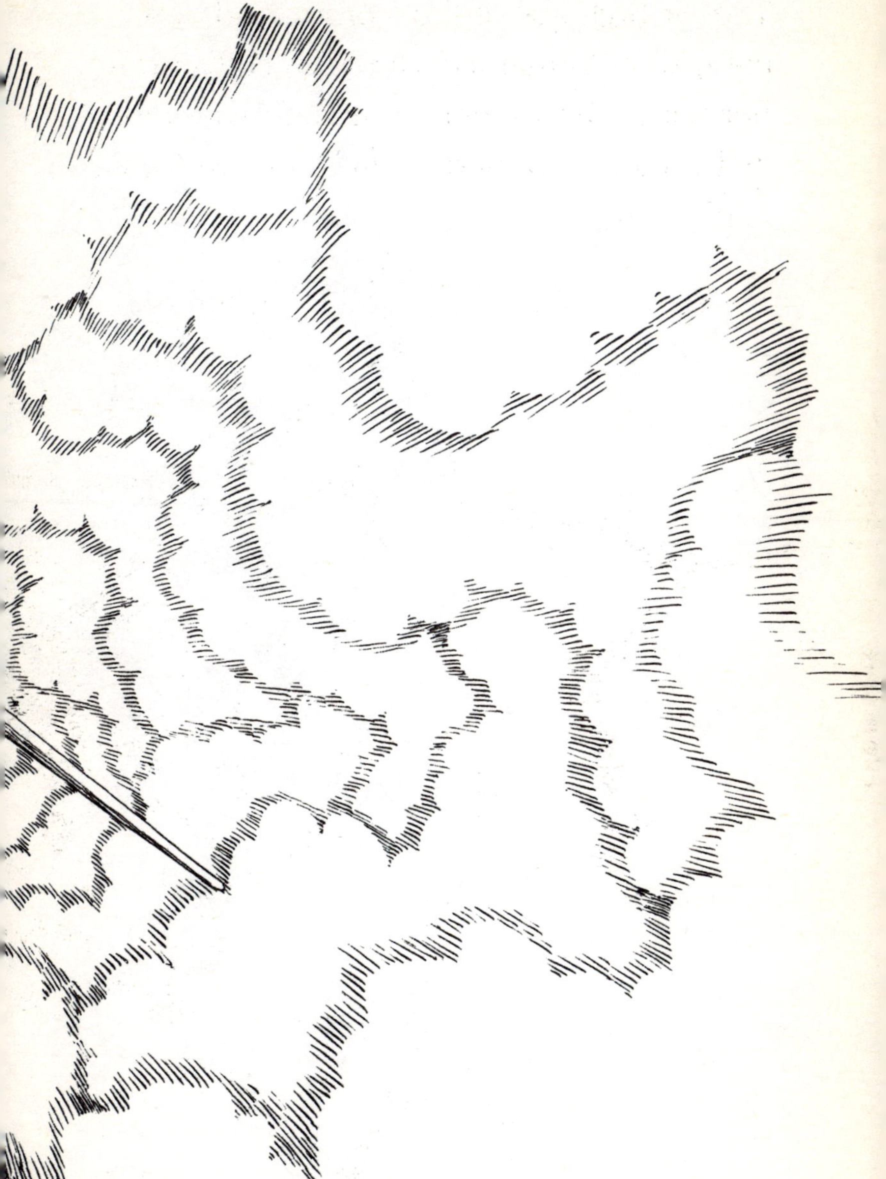

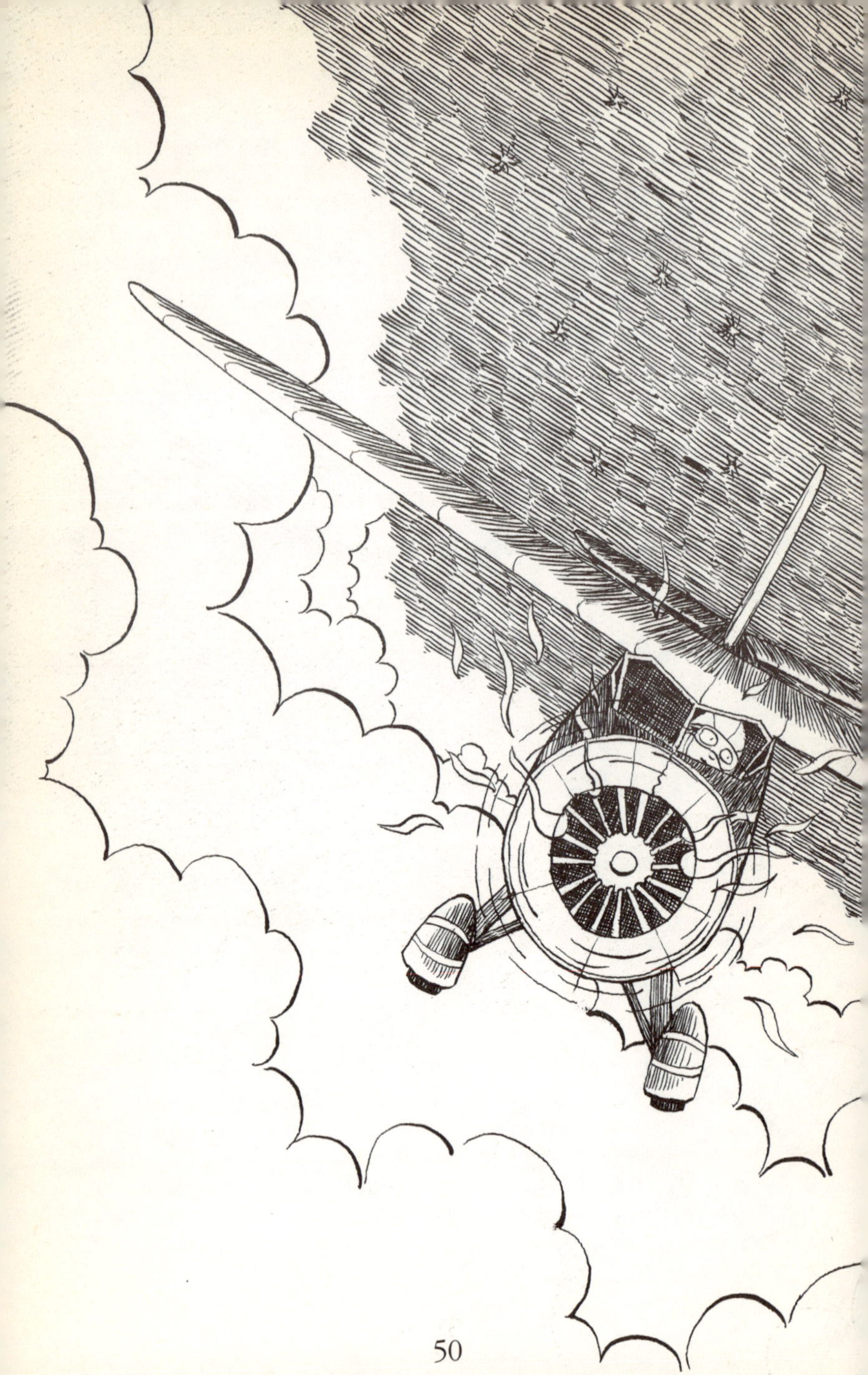

Amelia concentrated with every inch of her body and finally got the plane under control. She was still alive - but now the plane was badly damaged and fuel started to leak into the cockpit and trickle down her neck. She had no choice but to fly on, hoping the flames, still burning from her engine, wouldn't reach the fuel. If they did, the whole plane would explode!

Would the huge Atlantic ever end? Amelia flew on, desperate for land. Then at last the clouds started to clear, and in the sunshine Amelia could see a faint patch of green on the horizon.

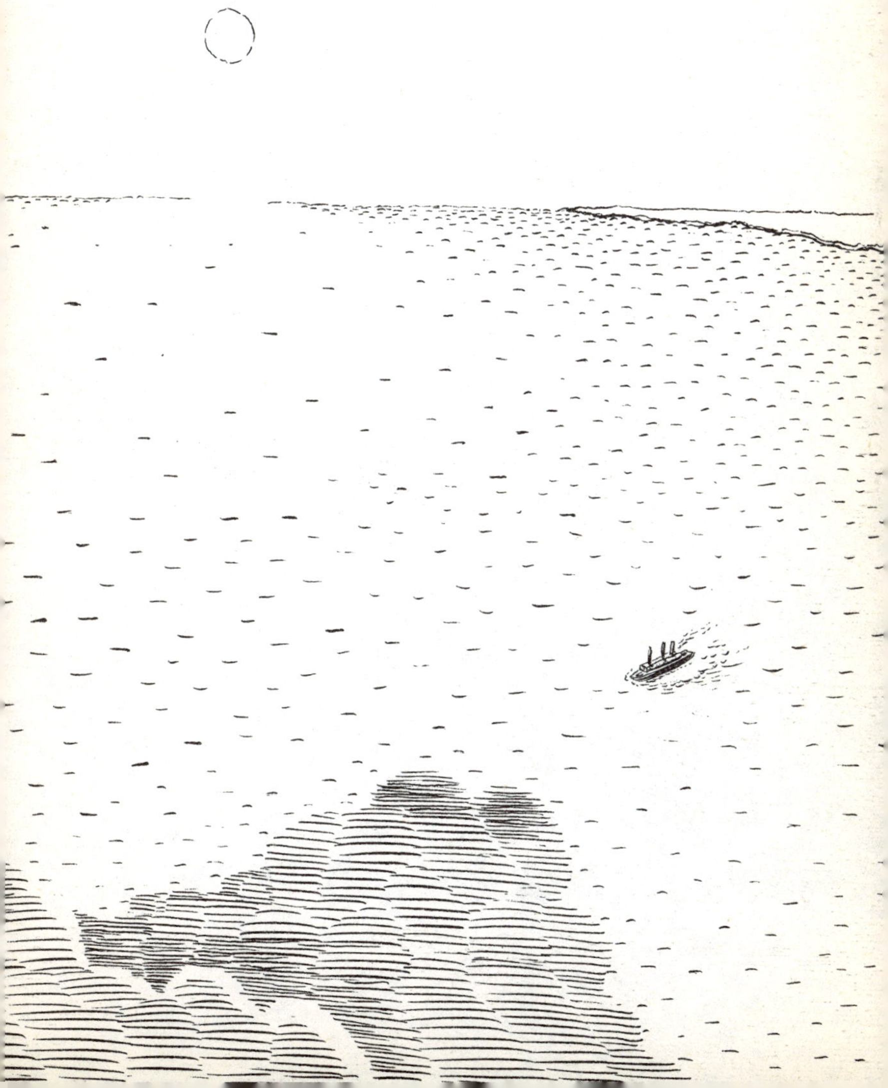

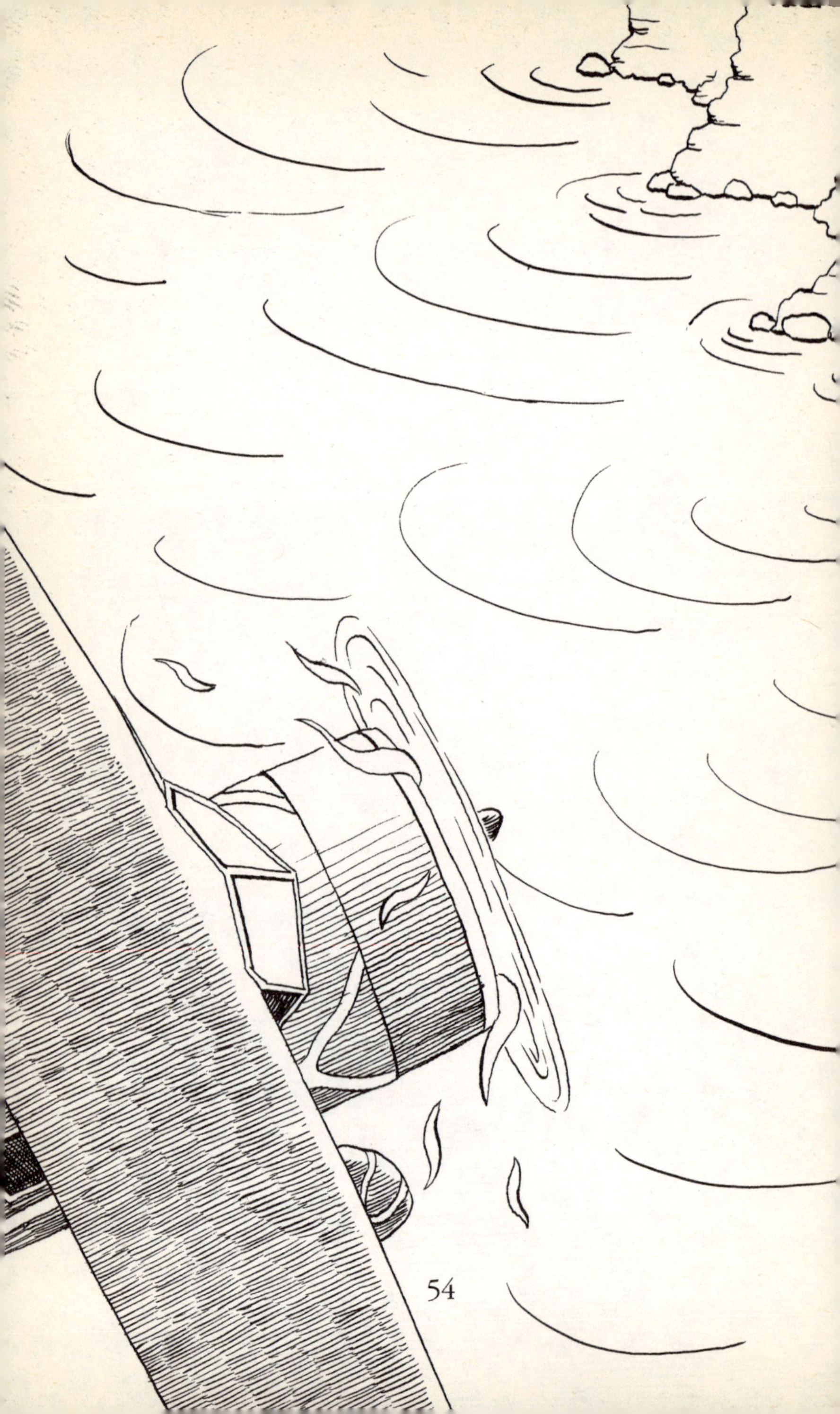

But her fuel was now very low, the plane was still in danger and she was exhausted. As the land came nearer and nearer, Amelia wondered if she would make it in time. She was so close, but now every second seemed to take an eternity.

56

Finally, the wheels of the plane touched the ground, and Amelia knew she was safe. She had set down in a cow paddock on a farm near Londonderry in Northern Ireland.

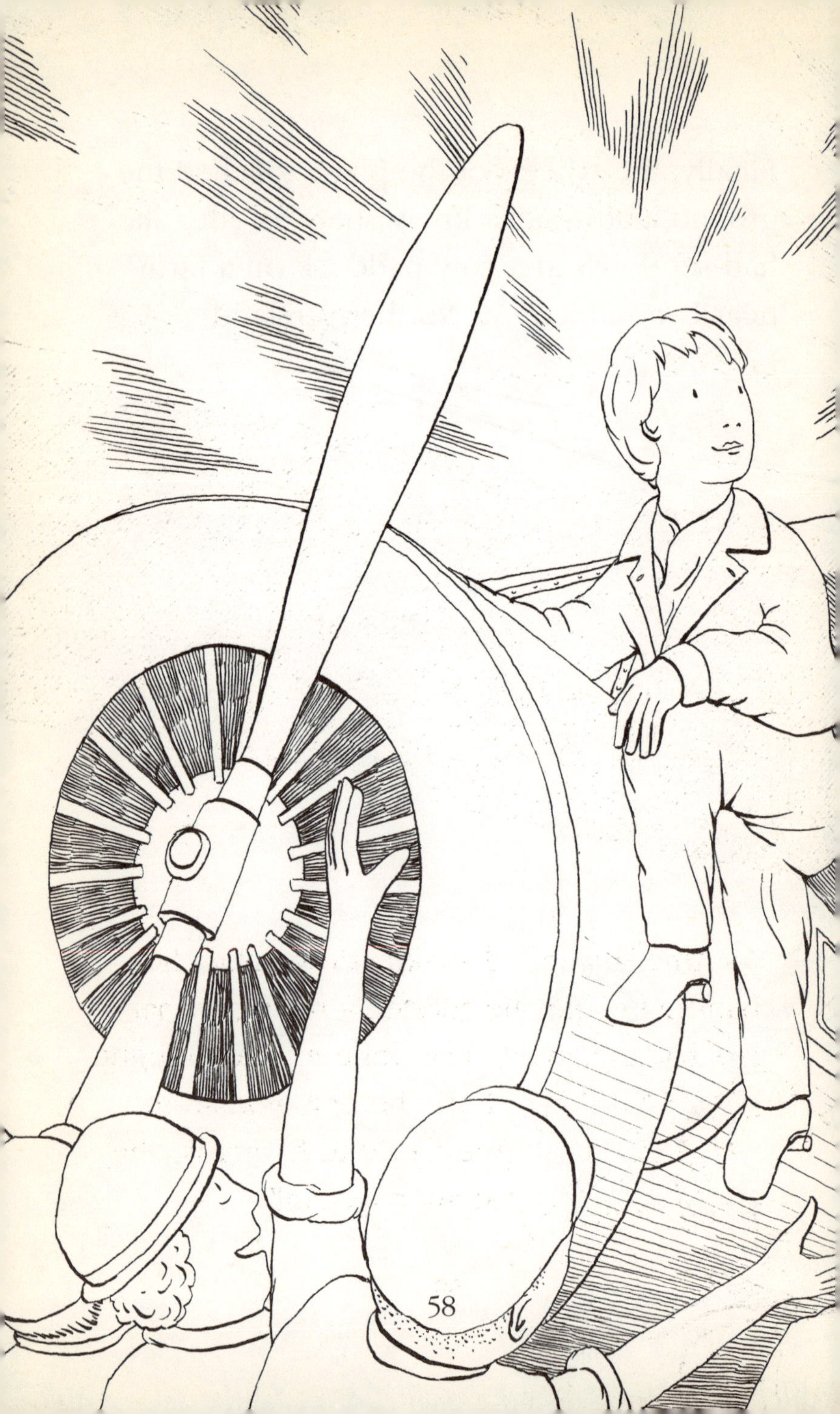

As Amelia stepped shakily down from her battered plane she suddenly realised what she had achieved. 'I've done it,' she thought. 'I am the first woman in the world to fly across the Atlantic Ocean!'

These days people fly everywhere. There are thousands of planes that each carry hundreds of people thousands of kilometres every day.

61

Amelia's brave Atlantic crossing took her 14 hours and 56 minutes and was full of dangers. If she flew from America to England today, it would take only about 6 hours, she could have a nap, and they would serve her lunch.

But somehow, I don't think she would enjoy it as much - do you?